THE
+BIG+
COUNT
DOWN
× + = −

Ten Thousand, Eight Hundred and Twenty Endangered Species in the Animal Kingdom

PAUL ROCKETT

W
FRANKLIN WATTS
LONDON • SYDNEY

Franklin Watts
This edition published in 2016 by
The Watts Publishing Group

Editor: Rachel Cooke
Design and illustration: Mark Ruffle
www.rufflebrothers.com

Dewey number: 591.6'8
ISBN: 978 1 4451 4740 6

Printed in China

Franklin Watts
An imprint of
Hachette Children's Group
Part of The Watts Publishing Group
Carmelite House
50 Victoria Embankment
London EC4Y 0DZ

An Hachette UK Company.

www.hachette.co.uk
www.franklinwatts.co.uk

*Every attempt has been made to clear copyright.
Should there be any inadvertent omission please
apply to the publisher for rectification.*

Picture credits: Christopher Ames/istockphoto:
22c; Antagain/istockphoto: 22cr; Beyond Images/
istockphoto: 23c; Jim Breakell/Shutterstock: front cover
b; Vittorio Bruno/Shutterstock: front cover c; Kenneth
Williams Caleno/Shutterstock: 22bl; Cameramannz/
Shutterstock: 11t; Carolina Biological/Visuals
Unlimited/Corbis: 29b; Carolina Biological/Visuals
Unllimited Inc/SPL: 17b; Mark Caunt/Shutterstock:
front cover t; Gerald & Butt Corsi/Corbis: 16bl; Lucca
Cranberry/istockphoto: 26cr; Cuson/Shutterstock: 19tr.
Lee Dalton/Photoshot: 29t; Eric Dragesco/Biosphotos/
FLPA: 19tc; Encicat/Shutterstock: 13cl, 24bl; James A
Harris/Shutterstock: 27br; Shawn Hempel/Shutterstock:
27tl; Hung Chung Chih/Shutterstock: 19tl; Imageman/
Shutterstock: 26tr; J4r3k/istockphoto: 15t; Kojihirano/
istockphoto: 13br; Konmesa/Shutterstock: 19br;
krechet/Shutterstock: 19bl; Anna Kucherova/
Shutterstock: 13cr; kzww/Shutterstock: 8b; Simon
Littlejohn/Foto Natura/Minden Pictures/Corbis: 13bl;
loflo69/Shutterstock: 18cr; loonger/istockphoto: 6tr;
Janelle Lugge/Shutterstock: 17bc; Pauline S Mills/
istockphoto: 22br; Michael Moffet/Minden Pictures/
FLPA: 28tl; Christian Musat/Shutterstock: 18bc;
Sean Nel/Shutterstock: 5t; Nicku/Shutterstock: 14tr;
Outdoorsman/Shutterstock: 18bl; Paul Rackham/
Alamy: 6tl; 2009fotofriends/Shutterstock: 14tc; Sergey
Uryadnikov/Shutterstock: 21tl; Kristina Vackova/
Shutterstock: 27bl; CC.Wikipedia Commons/ZooKeys:
8c; Worldwildlifewonders/Shutterstock:17bl.

**Throughout the book you are given data relating
to various pieces of information covering the topic.
The numbers will most likely be an estimation based
on research made over a period of time and in a
particular area. Some other research may reach
a different set of data, and all these figures may
change with time as new research and information
is gathered. The numbers provided within this book
are believed to be correct at the time of printing
and have been sourced from the following sites:**
*a-z-animals.com; anecdotage.com; animaldiscovery.
com; animals.nationalgeographic.co.uk;
animalkingdom.net; animals.about.com; arod.
com; articles.latimes.com; athene.as.arizona.edu;
backyardnature.net; bbc.co.uk; biologicaldiversity.
org; biologyjunction.com; britannica.com;
cotswoldwildlifepark.co.uk; currentresults.com;
darwin-online.org; eden.uktv.co.uk; eleaid.com;
enchantedlearning.com; eol.org; flseagrant.ifas.ufl.
edu; goldiesroom.org; greatbear.org; instruct.uwo.ca;
iucnredlist.org; jeb.biologists.org; kids.sandiegozoo.
org; library.thinkquest.org; news.nationalgeographic.
co.uk; nhm.ac.uk; pbrc.hawaii.edu; scienceclarified.
com; sciencedaily.com; sciencemag.org; seaworld.org;
snakesarelong.blogspot.co.uk; someinterestingfacts.
net; sussex-ifca.gov.uk; theanimalspot.com; tolweb.
org; txfossils.com; understanddolphins.tripod.com;
xterm-sumitomo.com.*

THE BIG COUNTDOWN
TEN THOUSAND, EIGHT HUNDRED AND TWENTY ENDANGERED SPECIES IN THE ANIMAL KINGDOM

CONTENTS

COUNTING DOWN THE ANIMAL KINGDOM

All living things on Earth are divided into five kingdoms. These kingdoms are groups of life forms that share similar characteristics in how they live.

LARGEST KINGDOM

The animal kingdom is almost three times larger than all of the other kingdoms put together. It includes the most varied and complex organisms on Earth. They need to eat and breathe to stay alive, they can move around freely, and range in size and form from a tiny flea to a giant whale.

THE FIVE KINGDOMS

Animals

Bacteria

Protists

Fungi

Plants

A colony of ants A gaggle of geese An army of frogs  A pack of dogs

HUMANS

Humans are the most dominant life form of the animal kingdom. They have developed means of survival that have given them the widest distribution across all environments, living all across the world. Humans have shown an interest in all forms of life, discovering and investigating how different creatures live, counting and categorising them.

Endangered animals, like these African penguins, are often tagged to track their location.

ZOOLOGY

Zoology is the study of the animal kingdom. Zoologists look at the biology, environment, behaviour and classification of all animals whether alive or extinct.

One of the important things zoologists do is tag animals with a computer chip which allows them to follow an animal's development, its movements and behaviour. Tagging is especially useful if that animal population is in decline, allowing zoologists to keep track of numbers and study possible threats. Farmers often tag their livestock as well, to keep track of their numbers.

NAMING GROUPS OF ANIMALS

Groups of animals that are not easily counted, or where the exact number is not needed, are often named with various collective nouns.

A group of birds is called 'a flock of birds'.

Animals that have four legs and like to graze are described as being part of a 'herd'. You can have a herd of bison, antelope, elephants, cows and goats.

A collection of fish is called 'a school of fish'.

THERE ARE SIGNS OF ANIMAL LIFE FROM 1,000,000,000 YEARS AGO

Fossils are the remains or impressions of a creature's body found in rocks. Fossils have revealed the existence of invertebrate animals that were alive around **600,000,000 years ago**.

BURROW TRACKS FOSSILISED ON ROCK

Scientists have found fossils of animal traces, such as burrowing tracks, that date back even further: over **1,000,000,000 years**. It is believed that these fossils are signs of creatures that had soft bodies with no skeleton, teeth or hard shell, and so the tracks are all we know of their existence.

FOSSIL OF A LIZARD FROM AROUND 145,000,000 YEARS AGO

PRECAMBRIAN ERA

PALEOZOIC ERA

OLDEST PROKARYOTIC FOSSILS 3,500,000,000 years ago

OXYGEN BEGINS TO ACCUMULATE IN THE ATMOSPHERE 2,500,000,000 years ago

O_2

SIMPLE MULTICELLULAR ORGANISMS EVOLVE 700,000,000 years ago

FIRST INSECTS 360,000,000 years ago

FIRST FISH 530,000,000 years ago

TIME (millions of years ago)

Prokaryotics, such as bacteria, are largely unicellular organisms, which means that they are composed of **one cell**. Many scientists suspect that prokaryotics were alive not long after the Earth's crust formed, which could mean that they have existed for over **4,500,000,000 years**.

OLDEST EUKARYOTIC FOSSILS 2,100,000,000 years ago

Eukaryotes are the first organisms that contain a nucleus and surrounding membrane.

INVERTEBRATES APPEAR 600,000,000 years ago

540,000,000

AMPHIBIANS APPEAR 370,000,000 years ago

REPTILES APPEAR 340,000,000 years ago

For a period of **183,000,000 years**, dinosaurs dominated the Earth. These were reptiles that roamed the land. Many of the dinosaurs were much larger than the animals on Earth today.

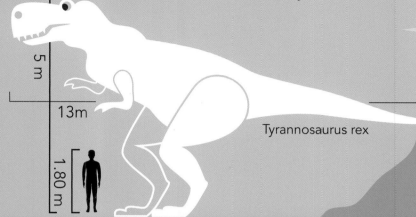

5 m

13m

1.80 m

Tyrannosaurus rex

No one is entirely sure how the dinosaurs died out. Some scientists think a huge meteorite crashed into the Earth or a giant volcano erupted, both creating a thick cloud of dust over the Earth. This cloud would have blocked out the Sun, preventing plant food from growing, with the dinosaurs finally starving to death.

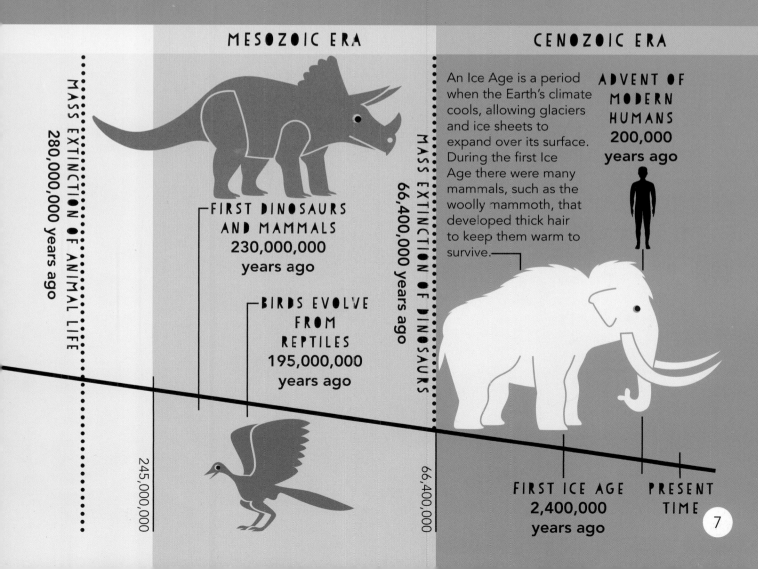

MESOZOIC ERA

CENOZOIC ERA

MASS EXTINCTION OF ANIMAL LIFE
280,000,000 years ago

MASS EXTINCTION OF DINOSAURS
66,400,000 years ago

An Ice Age is a period when the Earth's climate cools, allowing glaciers and ice sheets to expand over its surface. During the first Ice Age there were many mammals, such as the woolly mammoth, that developed thick hair to keep them warm to survive.

ADVENT OF MODERN HUMANS
200,000 years ago

FIRST DINOSAURS AND MAMMALS
230,000,000 years ago

BIRDS EVOLVE FROM REPTILES
195,000,000 years ago

245,000,000

66,400,000

FIRST ICE AGE
2,400,000 years ago

PRESENT TIME

THERE ARE 1,305,250 KNOWN INVERTEBRATES IN THE WORLD

An estimated 97% of all animal species are invertebrates. There are **1,305,250 known invertebrate species** alive today, with some scientists believing that there are many millions more yet to be discovered.

WHAT IS AN INVERTEBRATE?
Invertebrates are creatures without backbones. They are also cold-bloodied creatures, which means that they are unable to generate their own warmth, absorbing heat from their surroundings.

ARTHROPODS
Arthropods are the largest group of animals. It's estimated that **80%** of all animals on Earth are arthropods. These include ants, beetles, butterflies, grasshoppers, fleas, crabs, spiders and scorpions.

Arthropods' bodies are made up of sections and are covered by a shell or hard outer skin, called an exoskeleton. An exoskeleton is an external skeleton. Athropods have **six or more legs**. The anthropod with the most number of legs is the millipede. They have on average between **80-400 legs**.

A rare species of millipede, the *illacme plenipes*, has up to **750 legs**.

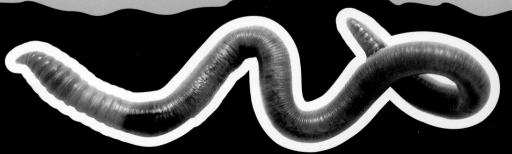

ANNELIDS
Annelids include earthworms and leeches. The have legless bodies made up of ring-shaped segments.

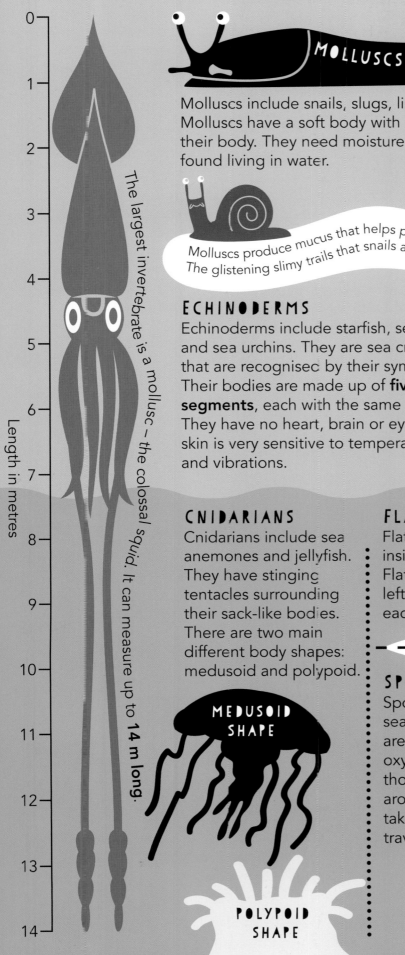

MOLLUSCS

Molluscs include snails, slugs, limpets, oysters, squid and octopus. Molluscs have a soft body with a hard shell either outside or inside their body. They need moisture in order to survive, and most can be found living in water.

Molluscs produce mucus that helps protect the soft parts of their body. The glistening slimy trails that snails and slugs leave behind is a track of this mucus.

ECHINODERMS

Echinoderms include starfish, sea cucumbers and sea urchins. They are sea creatures that are recognised by their symmetry. Their bodies are made up of **five identical segments**, each with the same set of organs. They have no heart, brain or eyes, but their skin is very sensitive to temperature, light and vibrations.

CNIDARIANS

Cnidarians include sea anemones and jellyfish. They have stinging tentacles surrounding their sack-like bodies. There are two main different body shapes: medusoid and polypoid.

MEDUSOID SHAPE

POLYPOID SHAPE

FLATWORMS

Flatworms live in the sea and also live inside the bodies of other animals. Flatworms have soft, flat bodies. The left and right sides are mirror images of each other.

SPONGES

Sponges are creatures that live on the seabed. They don't have any organs, but are covered in holes that let in food and oxygen. Most stay stuck to the seabed, though some travel incredibly slowly, at around **1 mm** distance per day. It would take a sponge around **2,739 years** to travel **1 km**.

The largest invertebrate is a mollusc – the colossal squid. It can measure up to **14 m long**.

Length in metres

9

THE LARGEST VERTEBRATE IS 33,000 MM LONG

Vertebrates make up about 3% of all animal species; the remaining 97% are invertebrates. Vertebrates are a group of animals that have backbones. They are divided into five groups:

BIRDS

AMPHIBIANS

REPTILES

FISH

MAMMALS

There are over **500,000 known vertebrates**, split across their groups as follows:

19.3%	10.4%	15.4%	45.3%	9.6%

← **100% OF VERTEBRATE SPECIES** →

FISH
Fish were the first animals to grow backbones. They are cold-blooded water animals that breathe by filtering oxygen from water through organs called gills.

There are **three groups** of fish:
1. Cartilaginous fish: includes sharks and rays
2. Lobe-finned fish: includes lungfish and coelacanths
3. Ray-finned fish: includes salmon and electric eels.

AMPHIBIANS
Amphibians are the first four-limbed vertebrates, and the first land animals to have evolved from fish. They are cold-blooded, live in water and on land and are capable of laying a large number of eggs. Amphibians are divided into **three groups**:
1. Newts and salamanders
2. Frogs and toads
3. Caecilians.

BIRDS
All birds have feathers, are warm-blooded, with **two legs** and **two wings,** and the females lay eggs. There are **30 bird groups**, including raptors, songbirds and cranes.

REPTILES

TUATARA

Reptiles are cold-blooded, scaly animals that live on land. The majority of reptiles lay eggs, and have either **four legs** or no legs.

Reptiles are divided into **four groups**:

1. Turtles: includes terrapins and tortoises
2. Squamata: includes lizards and snakes
3. Crocodilians: includes alligators and crocodiles
4. Tuataras: only includes the tuatara.

MAMMALS

Mammals are warm-bloodied and hairy, and feed their babies with milk from their bodies.

Although a sea creature, the whale is a mammal. Like other mammals, they breathe in oxygen directly from the air. However, whales don't breathe through their mouth but through a blowhole at the top of their head. When a blue whale exhales, a spray of water comes out which can reach up to **9 m** high.

The blue whale lives off tiny shrimp-like creatures called krill. It's known that in a single day they may consume over **3 tonnes** of krill.

The world's largest animal is a mammal: the **blue whale**.

That figure can also be represented as:

The blue whale can grow to **33,000 mm long**. **3,300 cm or 33 m.**

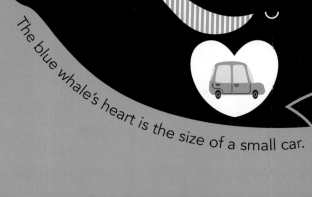

The blue whale's heart is the size of a small car.

10,820 ENDANGERED SPECIES IN THE ANIMAL KINGDOM

Many animal populations are so small that they face a threat of extinction. Three main threats to all animal species are: habitat loss, climate change and poaching.

HABITAT LOSS

This includes the destruction of natural animal homes, usually through industrialisation and farming. This is currently a threat to **85%** of all animal species.

CLIMATE CHANGE

Through increased industrialisation, humans have contributed to an over-production of carbon dioxide causing the Earth's temperature to rise. This increase in temperature has affected climate and weather patterns, impacting on the rhythms of animal life.

The changes in temperature have affected the nesting conditions of the loggerhead turtle causing a great imbalance in the male to female ratio. As a result there are **nine females for every one male**.

80%

80% of orangutans have disappeared over the last **100 years**, largely from logging and the clearing of forests for palm oil plantations.

POACHING

Many animals are hunted for sport, as trophies or for medicines.

Hunting halved the elephant population between 1981–89.

VULNERABLE TO EXTINCTION

The International Union for the Conservation of Nature took a sample of **49,826 known animal species** and found that **10,820** of these were at threat of extinction. These animals were placed in the following categories:

Vulnerable: High risk of endangerment in the wild	5,297
Endangered: High risk of extinction in the wild	3,262
Critically endangered: Extremely high risk of extinction in the wild	2,261
Extinct in the wild: Known only to survive in captivity	32
Extinct: No known individuals remaining	705

ANIMALS AT THREAT

33% INVERTEBRATES

67% VERTEBRATES

Out of the **10,820 animals** at threat of extinction **7,250** are vertebrates and **3,570** are invertebrates.

VERTEBRATES AT THREAT

Mammals: **20%**
Birds: **10%**
Reptiles: **21%**
Amphibians: **30%**
Fish: **19%**

VULNERABLE: KOMODO DRAGON

Measuring **3 m in length**, it is the largest living species of lizard.
Location: islands of Indonesia
Population: approximately **5,000** living in the wild
Threat: loss of habitat, loss of prey, poaching

ENDANGERED: BENGAL TIGER

Location: India with small populations in Bangladesh, Nepal, China and Myanmar.
Population: approximately **2,500** in the wild
Threat: poaching

CRITICALLY ENDANGERED: CALIFORNIA CONDOR

Became extinct in the wild in 1987. **22 remaining birds** were captured, bred in captivity and released in the wild in 1991.
Location: North America
Population: 405 (**226** in wild, **179** in captivity)
Threat: poaching, lead poisoning, habitat destruction

EXTINCT: PYRENEAN IBEX

Location: The Pyrenees mountains of France and Spain
Last sighting: 2000
Extinct: Believed to have died out through poaching and inability to compete with other species for food. In 2009, an attempt was made by scientists to make the Pyrenean ibex 'unextinct' through cloning. However, a clone died just **seven minutes** after it was born. No further attempts have been made.

13

DARWIN HAD 10,000 BARNACLES IN HIS HOME

Charles Darwin was a naturalist whose ideas about evolution changed the way people understand life on Earth.

In 1831, at the age of 22, Darwin set sail in the ship the HMS *Beagle*. This was a survey ship that sailed around the world making maps of coastlines. Darwin went along to collect plant and animal specimens from the different islands that the ship would visit.

Charles Darwin, 1808–1882

BARNACLES

Darwin became an expert in barnacles, and was able to study them while sailing on HMS *Beagle*. Barnacles are arthropods that are closely related to crabs. They tend to live in shallow waters and attach themselves to rocks, ships and other animals. Darwin was so obsessed with barnacles, that he had over **10,000** in his home.

THE JOURNEY OF HMS *BEAGLE*

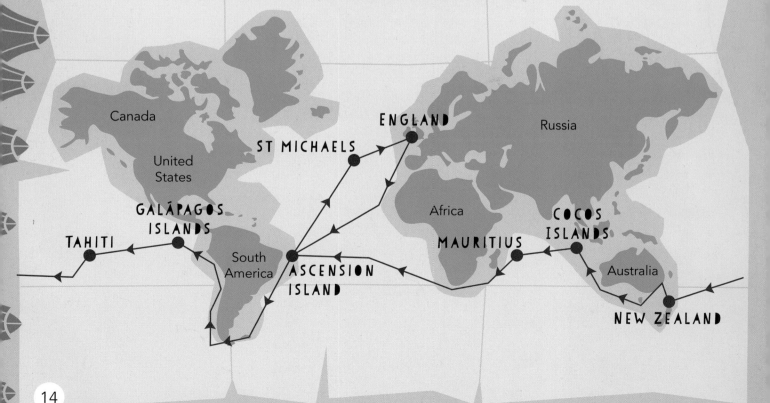

Canada
United States
ST MICHAELS
ENGLAND
Russia
GALÁPAGOS ISLANDS
TAHITI
South America
ASCENSION ISLAND
Africa
MAURITIUS
COCOS ISLANDS
Australia
NEW ZEALAND

THE GALÁPAGOS ISLANDS

On the Galápagos Islands, Darwin noticed that there were plants and animals that could not be found anywhere else in the world. He noticed that each of the Galápagos Islands was home to a giant tortoise and that it was possible through size and character to distinguish which tortoise came from which island.

On his return, Darwin also noticed that the finches from all of the islands were similar, but that on each island the finch had a different beak. These beaks had developed to crack the different hardness of nuts and to eat the various insects of the different islands.

Large ground finch

Medium ground finch

Small tree finch

Green warbler finch

ON THE ORIGIN OF SPECIES

Darwin noted that plants and animals change over time; they evolve, changing to adapt to their landscape and to ensure that they can find food. In 1859, he published his ideas in a book called *On the Origin of Species*. His book upset many people, including those in the Church, who believed that God had created all living things as perfect unchanging beings. However, his ideas revolutionised the way people think about animal life and how it adapts to survive.

Canthidium darwini dung beetle

Paraliochthonius darwini scorpion

Since the publication of his book, more than **120 species** have been named after him.

Phyllotis darwini mouse

Tapetosa darwini spider

Thecacera darwini sea slug

Calantica darwini barnacle

THE TERMITE QUEEN LAYS 2,000 EGGS A DAY

Animals go through lots of changes from the moment they are born until they die. The changes that occur during this period are called its life cycle.

VERTEBRATE LIFE CYCLE
Most vertebrates have a simple life cycle in **three stages:** ···········

An example of this would be a lion:

NEWBORN   **CUB**   **FULLY GROWN ADULT**

BIRTH
▼
YOUNG
▼
ADULT

BUTTERFLY LIFE CYCLE
Invertebrate life cycles are more complex and can include a period of metamorphosis. There are **four stages** in the life cycle of a butterfly:

Butterfly

Chrysalis

Egg

Caterpillar

JELLYFISH LIFE CYCLE
Jellyfish go through **five stages** in their life cycle:

Adult jellyfish

Eggs from inside an adult jellyfish hatch to release planula larva.

The topmost layer of polyps eventually comes free, as a tiny jellyfish, called an ephyra.

The larva drop to the bottom of the sea, attaching themselves to the sea bed, and become polyps.

The polyp grows more layers of polyps.

JELLYFISH POLYPS ········

EGGS

All animals begin life inside an egg. The fertilisation of an egg is the beginning of an animal's journey to life. The egg may stay inside their parent, or the egg may be laid into the world to continue its development before it hatches and the animal is born.

ALL BIRDS LAY EGGS

Ostriches lay the biggest bird egg. It can weigh up to **1.5 kilograms**. The smallest bird egg is laid by the bee hummingbird, and weighs around **half a gram**.

17

1

A grey partridge can lay **17 eggs** in succession.
A condor will lay **one egg** every **two years**.

1.5 kg

0.5 g

Whereas bird eggs have a hard shell to protect them, fish eggs are round and jelly-like.

An ocean sunfish can lay up to **300,000,000 eggs** at a time.

Cod can produce **4–6,000,000 eggs** at one time.

Eggs laid by invertebrates are mainly round and with a soft protective exterior. The termite queen lays **2,000 eggs a day**.

2 0 0 0

PLATYPUS

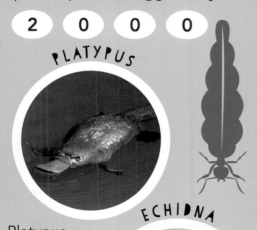

ECHIDNA

Platypus and echidna are the only mammals that lay eggs.

GESTATION PERIODS

Most mammals give birth to live young. Before being born, the baby will go through what is called a gestation period. This is the period of development in which they form their body parts. Different animals have different periods of gestation.

A developing human baby at 40 days

The average gestation period of a human is **nine months**.

The mammal with the shortest gestation period is the opossum, lasting **12 days**.

The mammal with the longest gestation period is the elephant, lasting **645 days**.

1,600 GIANT PANDAS IN THE FORESTS OF CHINA

A habitat is a type of environment in which plants and animals live.

Animals live in habitats that suit their needs, providing them with food, water and shelter.

SIX MAIN HABITATS

The main habitats in order from the one containing the most species to the one containing the least:

Rainforest | Marine | Forest | Grassland | Desert

Polar

Habitat with the smallest population of animal species: polar

ADAPTING TO HABITATS

Animal species are able to adapt to their habitats in order to survive. Unlike other bear species, the polar bear is an excellent swimmer. It has adapted to travel in the water and on land. This is necessary for it to search for food in its frozen sea habitat.

BEAR HABITATS

There are **eight species** of bear, all living in different habitats across the world.

Arctic

USA

Bear: polar bear
Habitat: polar
Diet: seals
Population: 20,000–25,000

Bear: American black bear
Habitat: forests
Diet: berries, nuts, ants, fish
Population: 950,000

Andes, South America

Bear: spectacled bear
Habitat: forests
Diet: cactus, sugarcane, llama
Population: unknown

THE YETI BEAR?

For centuries there have been tales about an ape-like creature that lives in the mountains of the Himalayas. Known as the yeti or the Abominable Snowman, its existence is accounted for by a few sightings and some blurred photos. In 2013, scientists tested some hair samples believed to be those of a yeti. They found DNA similar to that of a polar bear. In fact, they believe that the mysterious creature in the mountains may well be a new species or hybrid of bear.

Brown bears lived in Britain until around 1000 CE, when they were wiped out through over hunting.

BROWN BEAR

The brown bear is the most widely distributed bear species across the world. There are around **200,000 brown bears** living in Europe, Russia, North America and parts of Asia.

Bear: giant panda
Habitat: forest
Diet: bamboo
Population: 1,600

Bear: Gobi bear
(subspecies of the
brown bear)
Habitat: desert
Diet: roots, berries
Population: 22–31

Bear: Sun bear
Habitat: rainforest
Diet: bees, termites
Population: unknown

KOALA BEARS

Koala bears are not bears, but marsupials, which are mammals that have a pouch in which they carry their newborn.

Gobi Desert

China

Japan

India

Southeast Asia Thailand

Bear: sloth bear
Habitat: grasslands
Diet: termites, fruit
Population: 20,000

Bear: Asian black bear
Habitat: forests
Diet: termites, fish, rodents
Population: 28,000

Animals will often travel large distances in order to find food, shelter, and a good place to reproduce, lay their eggs or give birth. This is known as 'migration' and mainly occurs seasonally, with the changing weather encouraging animals to travel to where the temperature is more suited to their survival.

Migration may occur only once in an animal's lifetime, as with the monarch butterfly, or it may occur many times, as it does for the Arctic tern.

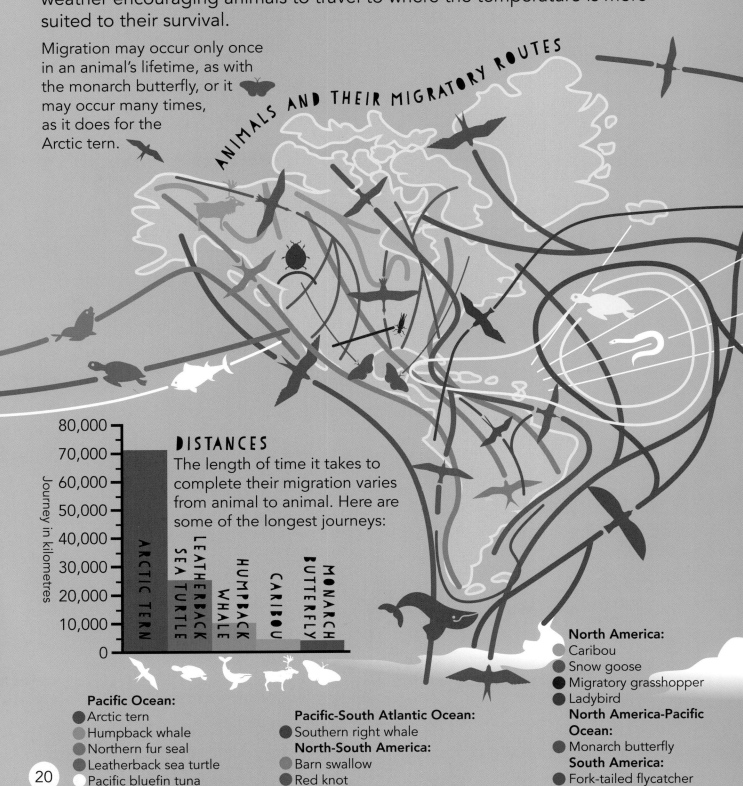

ANIMALS AND THEIR MIGRATORY ROUTES

DISTANCES

The length of time it takes to complete their migration varies from animal to animal. Here are some of the longest journeys:

Journey in kilometres

80,000
70,000
60,000
50,000
40,000
30,000
20,000
10,000
0

ARCTIC TERN
LEATHERBACK SEA TURTLE
HUMPBACK WHALE
CARIBOU
MONARCH BUTTERFLY

Pacific Ocean:
- Arctic tern
- Humpback whale
- Northern fur seal
- Leatherback sea turtle
- Pacific bluefin tuna

Pacific-South Atlantic Ocean:
- Southern right whale

North-South America:
- Barn swallow
- Red knot

North America:
- Caribou
- Snow goose
- Migratory grasshopper
- Ladybird

North America-Pacific Ocean:
- Monarch butterfly

South America:
- Fork-tailed flycatcher

THE ARCTIC TERN

The Arctic tern travels from its breeding grounds in the Arctic to Antarctica. Its route ensures that it sees **two summers** per year and means that it sees more daylight than any other creature on the planet. It can live for over **30 years**, during which time it will have travelled an equivalent distance of **three return journeys** to the Moon.

X3

Some animals only need to travel over much shorter distances to maintain their survival. In the Yosemite National Park, in the USA, ladybirds will migrate **321 km** over the mountains to find shelter for winter hibernation.

Atlantic Ocean:
- Arctic tern
- Wilson's storm petrel
- Loggerhead sea turtle
- Red-necked phalarope
- European eel

Eurasia:
- Red knot
- Eurasian barn swallow

Europe:
- Snowy owl
- European goldfinch

Africa:
- White-bearded wildebeest
- African brown veined butterfly
- Locust
- **Asia:** Siberian white crane

THE CHEETAH CAN TRAVEL UP TO 112 KM PER HOUR

Animals need to move to escape danger, find food and stay healthy.

FLYING AND GLIDING

Some animals depend on wind pressure and air flow to help them fly and glide through the air. The wind is caught in their wings or flaps of skin, holding them aloft.

THE LONGEST RECORDED GLIDE OF A FLYING SQUIRREL IS 90 METRES.

Most birds, winged insects and bats power their flight by pushing themselves through the air, flapping their wings. Birds have different shaped wings that allow them to fly in different ways. Some are designed to glide more, fly high, or fly at great speed.

VARIED THRUSH
Elliptical wings allow for tight, short, quick movements in confined spaces.

SWALLOW
Fast birds have high-speed wings. The wings are also shaped to allow the wind to travel past with little drag, allowing for high-speed diving.

ALBATROSS
Birds with soaring wings use air currents to stay in the sky, minimising their flapping to save energy.

HAWK
High-lift wings are used for controlled flights, allowing birds to study small areas of land or sea for their prey.

WALKING

Animals walk by lifting their feet, taking steps in order to move forwards. How they do this depends on the number of legs they have.

TWO LEGS
Move by putting one leg forwards, then the other leg.

SIX LEGS
Move with one leg on one side of their body and two on the other side at the same time.

FOUR LEGS
Usually travel with diagonally opposite legs moving at the same time.

MANY LEGS
Lift one pair of legs, then the pair behind and so on, moving in a wave-like motion.

LEAPING

Many animals make long and high leaps to travel from place to place, get food or escape predators.

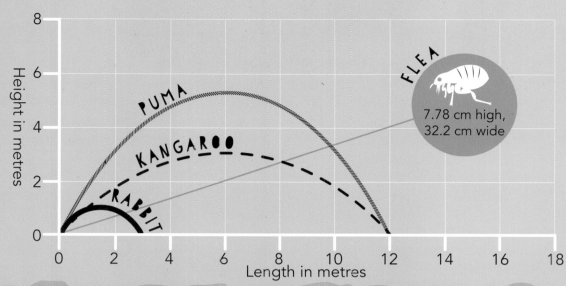

FLEA
7.78 cm high, 32.2 cm wide

PUMA

KANGAROO

RABBIT

Height in metres: 0, 2, 4, 6, 8

Length in metres: 0, 2, 4, 6, 8, 10, 12, 14, 16, 18

CRAWLING AND BURROWING

Animals that crawl move by dragging themselves along, using their muscles to push different parts of their body against the ground to move forwards. Snakes do this by stretching and tightening different parts of their body at the same time, moving along in S-shaped curves. On land, leeches use suckers that help drag them along.

Animals that burrow underground also use the muscles in the body to push them through, or if they have arms and legs they use them as paddles to dig through the dirt.

SWIMMING

Underwater animals propel themselves forwards in different ways. Most fish have fins that push them forwards, navigate their direction and balance. They are also streamlined which allows them to move through the water with little friction or drag.

ROWING

Some animals use legs, or tiny hairs that move back and forth like oars, pushing them forwards.

SQUIRTING

Some animals, like jellyfish and squid, take water into their bodies, then squirt it out quickly, propelling them along.

BENDING

Some sea animals bend in an S-shape that pushes them forwards.

FASTEST ANIMALS

Some of the fastest animals are predators that are able to increase their speed for short bursts in order to catch their prey.

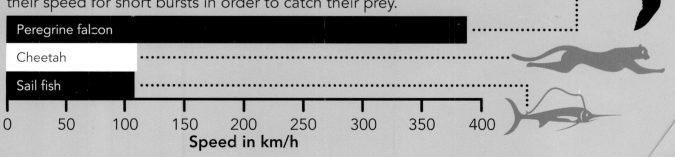

Peregrine falcon

Cheetah

Sail fish

Speed in km/h: 0, 50, 100, 150, 200, 250, 300, 350, 400

Every habitat has its own food chain, or series of food chains.
A food chain shows the eating habits of animals. It tells you which animals eat each other and shows how a habitat's ecosystem is kept in balance.

FOOD CHAIN OF AN OWL

FOOD CHAIN OF A POLAR BEAR

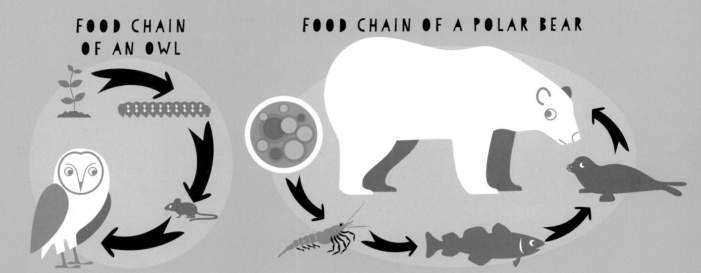

TEETH

Animals' teeth are different depending upon what foods they eat. Animals that eat meat have sharp teeth; those that eat only plants have flat teeth.

 Animals that eat only plants are called herbivores.

Animals that eat both plants and meat are called omnivores.

Animals that eat mainly meat are called carnivores.

CARNIVORE'S TEETH

HERBIVORE'S TEETH

Humans have 32 teeth
Their front teeth are sharp for biting, whilst the back teeth are flat for chewing.

Giraffes have 32 teeth
Their teeth are grooved to help strip leaves from branches.

Hippopotami have 40 teeth
Their front teeth are used for fighting, whilst their flat back teeth are used for chewing grass.

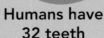

Crocodiles have 60 teeth
Their teeth grasp and tear at the flesh of other animals.

Dolphins have 250 teeth
Their teeth help pick up sounds to locate and trap prey.

Snails have 25,600 teeth
Their tiny teeth scrape off food from plants.

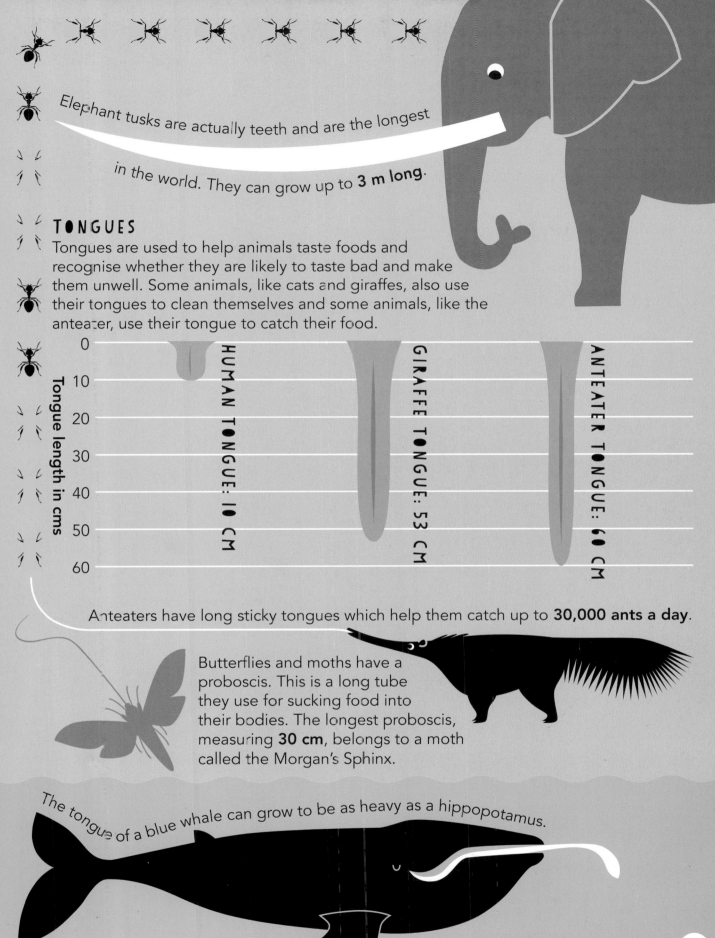

Elephant tusks are actually teeth and are the longest in the world. They can grow up to **3 m long**.

TONGUES

Tongues are used to help animals taste foods and recognise whether they are likely to taste bad and make them unwell. Some animals, like cats and giraffes, also use their tongues to clean themselves and some animals, like the anteater, use their tongue to catch their food.

Tongue length in cms

| 0 | 10 | 20 | 30 | 40 | 50 | 60 |

HUMAN TONGUE: 10 CM

GIRAFFE TONGUE: 53 CM

ANTEATER TONGUE: 60 CM

Anteaters have long sticky tongues which help them catch up to **30,000 ants a day**.

Butterflies and moths have a proboscis. This is a long tube they use for sucking food into their bodies. The longest proboscis, measuring **30 cm**, belongs to a moth called the Morgan's Sphinx.

The tongue of a blue whale can grow to be as heavy as a hippopotamus.

THE PINK FLAMINGO HAS 12 BLACK FEATHERS

Animal bodies are covered in skin, hair, feathers, scales or shells, all designed to keep them warm, cool, dry or moist and protect them in their habitats.

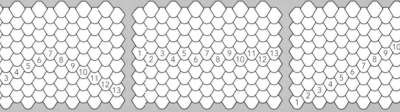

THE SCALES OF A ROACH FISH

SCALES

Fish have moist scales as do reptiles that spend a lot of their time in the water. Reptiles that live mainly on land have dry scales.

Scales are small, hard plates that cover the body for protection and keep moisture inside the body. The scales overlap to form a flexible armour plating that helps to protect against predators and bruising.

Some species of snake can be identified by the number of scales in a row across their body.

Three different ways to count the number of scales.

AMPHIBIANS

The skin of amphibians is able to absorb water and oxygen and produces a mucus that stops their skin from drying out. The skin in some amphibians, such as poison arrow frogs, is also able to produce toxins to deter predators.

100,000 individual hairs per cm².

HAIR

All mammals have hair on their bodies – even whales. The hair may not grow all over the body and it may soon disappear after birth. Humans have a similar number of hairs to chimpanzees, but the hair is not as thick, long or dark.

Sea otters have a very thick coat of fur, with more than **100,000 individual hairs per cm²**.

FEATHERS

Birds are the only animals to have feathers. Feathers grow out from a bird's skin, much in the same way hair grows on a mammal. Feathers protect the skin from injury and help keep it dry.

Feathers are light and can be broad with a large lifting surface area that helps birds fly. Their tail feathers serve as rudders and help them balance when in flight.

Some birds' feathers have complex patterns and bright colours, often used to attract a mate.

The male peacock displays his tail feathers in a vertical fan during courtship.

Most songbirds have between **2,000 to 4,000 feathers**, of which **30 to 40%** are around the head and neck.

Figeons can have up to **1,600 feathers** around their head and neck.

Flamingoes are born with white feathers, gaining their pink and red colouring from the particular shrimp that they eat. The healthier they are the brighter their colouring. However, they have **12 black feathers** in each wing, which are their flight feathers.

SHELLS

Shells can be found on animals such as molluscs, sea urchins, crustaceans and turtles. Shells protect an animal from predators, contain their bodies and prevent them from drying out.

Gastropod molluscs, such as snails, have spirals that coil, either upwards or flat.

These spirals are counted in whorls.

1
2
3
whorls

Over **90%** of gastropods have shells that coil to the right, with under **10%** coiling to the left.

DEVIL SCORPIONFISH

CAMOUFLAGE

Most animals have developed camouflage, colours and patterns, that help them blend in to their natural environment, protecting them from predators.

ZEBRA

The black and white lines of the zebra blend in with the wavy lines of the tall grass around it. It doesn't matter that the stripes are black and white whereas the grass is green and yellow as its main predator, the lion, is colourblind.

The animal kingdom is home to creatures that can be too small for the naked eye to see as well as too big to take in up close.

GIANT WETA

0.25 mm

INSECTS

The largest recorded insect is the giant weta, found on Little Barrier Island, New Zealand. This cricket-like creature weighs the same as **three mice** and has a wingspan just under **18 cm**.

The smallest insect in the world is a fairyfly known as tinkerbell. Found in Costa Rica, the tinkerbell measures **0.25 mm** in length.

REPTILES

The longest reptile is the giant anaconda, found around the Amazon and Orinoco basins. It can grow up to **9 m long**. That's almost as long as a double-decker bus.

There are two reptiles that make claim to the title of smallest reptile: the Virgin Islands dwarf gecko and the dwarf gecko from the Dominican Republic. These measure **33 mm** in length and can fit on the end of a matchstick.

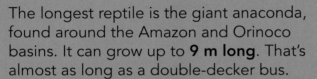

GIANT ANACONDA

x 273 DWARF GECKOS

MAMMALS

The longest mammal is the blue whale at **33 m**. The smallest mammal is the Kitti's hog-nosed bat, also known as the bumblebee bat. It would take **1,100** of these bats to match the length of the blue whale.

Found in Thailand, when fully-grown the Kitti's hog-nosed bat measures **3 cm** long with a wingspan of **12 cm**. It weighs the same as a small coin.

BIRDS

Not only is it the fastest bird on land, but the ostrich is also the largest bird, measuring **2.8 m** in height.

The smallest bird in the world is the male bee hummingbird, which lives in Cuba. It weighs **1.6 g** and is **6.98 cm** in length. The beak and tail make up half of his length.

2.8 m

FISH

The smallest known fish in the world is the *paedocypris progenetica*. It belongs to the carp family of fish and lives in the swamps of Sumatra in Indonesia. It measures between **7.9 to 10.33 mm** in length.

It would take over **12,000** of the smallest fish to line up alongside the largest fish. This is the whale shark, and it can measure up to **12.65 m** in length.

THE SMALLEST

Many zoologists believe that the myxozoa could be the smallest animal in the world. It is a worm-like aquatic parasite that lives off fish, such as trout. It ranges in size from **0.01 to 0.02 mm**.

FURTHER INFORMATION

BOOKS

Animal Encyclopedia (National Geographic Society, 2012)
Extraordinary Animals by Leon Gray (Wayland, 2013)
Very Wonderful, Very Rare by Marilyn and Jonathan Baillie
(Franklin Watts, 2013)
Wildlife Wonders series x 6 titles (Franklin Watts, 2014)

WEBSITES

Videos, games and photos providing profiles and information on all
animal forms:
ngkids.co.uk
Searchable database of a large selection of animals with fascinating facts:
kidsbiology.com/animals-for-children.php
Animal puzzles, quizzes and activities:
discoverykids.com/explore/

Note to parents and teachers:
Every effort has been made by the publisher to ensure that these websites contain no
inappropriate or offensive material. However, because of the nature of the Internet, it is
impossible to guarantee that the content of these sites will not be altered. We strongly
advise that Internet access is supervised by a responsible adult.

LARGE NUMBERS

1,000,000,000,000,000,000,000,000,000,000,000 = ONE DECILLION

1,000,000,000,000,000,000,000,000,000,000 = ONE NONILLION

1,000,000,000,000,000,000,000,000,000 = ONE OCTILLION

1,000,000,000,000,000,000,000,000 = ONE SEPTILLION

1,000,000,000,000,000,000,000 = ONE SEXTILLION

1,000,000,000,000,000,000 = ONE QUINTILLION

1,000,000,000,000,000 = ONE QUADRILLION

1,000,000,000,000 = ONE TRILLION

1,000,000,000 = ONE BILLION

1,000,000 = ONE MILLION

1000 = ONE THOUSAND

100 = ONE HUNDRED

10 = TEN

1 = ONE

amphibian	cold-blooded vertebrate that lives both on land and in water
annelid	invertebrate, such as an earthworm or leech, whose outer-body is built along ringed segments
arthropod	invertebrate with an external skeleton, including spiders and crabs
camouflage	colouring of an animal that enables it to blend in with its surroundings
cell	tiny structure that makes up all living things
climate change	change in the Earth's climate, especially through an increase in temperature in the atmosphere
cnidarian	invertebrate that mainly lives in the water, with stinging tentacles and a sack-like internal body, including sea anemones and jellyfish
collective noun	noun that is singular but refers to a group of things
DNA	material present in nearly all living organisms containing information essential to the understanding of each organism's make up
echinoderm	marine invertebrates that are symmetrical in form
ecosystem	community of organisms interacting within an environment
endangered	at risk of extinction (dying out)
exoskeleton	protective and supporting structure or shell covering the body of animals, especially invertebrates
extinct	having no living members; species that has died out
fertilisation	process by which animals and plants reproduce, creating a new individual life
fossil	remains or impression of a plant or animal hardened in rock
gastropod	mollusc, such as a snail or slug, that moves along by one large muscular foot
gestation	time during which an organism develops inside its mother before birth
habitat	the environment or home of a creature or plant
hibernation	to spend the period of winter sleeping or resting
hybrid	animal that is produced from two animals of different kinds
invertebrate	animal that does not have a backbone
mammal	warm-bloodied vertebrate
migration	movement to another place, often for a change of season
mollusc	invertebrate with a soft body and hard shell, such as snails and clams
multicellular	consisting of many cells
naturalist	someone who studies natural history (plants and animals)
origin	beginning or starting point where something was created
oxygen	gas that plants produce and animals breathe in to live
poaching	act of killing or taking wild animals illegally
predator	animal that kills other animals for its own survival
proboscis	long extended part of mouth or nose that aids breathing or eating, such as a tube for moths, or a trunk for elephants
reptile	cold-bloodied air-breathing vertebrate
species	living things that contain shared characteristics, e.g. human beings
specimen	something taken as an example of its larger being or group
termite	small ant-like insect that lives in groups
unicellular	consisting of a single cell
vertebrate	animal that has a backbone
zoology	scientific study of animals

INDEX